Copland for Flute

AARON COPLAND

BOOSEY & HAWKES

AN IMAGEM COMPANY

DISTRIBUTED BY

HAL•LEONARD®
CORPORATION

7777 W. BLUEMOUND RD. P.O. BOX 13819 MILWAUKEE, WI 53213

Foreword

It has been my pleasure to complete this set of solo books based on the music of Aaron Copland. Many of these solos were taken from his vocal works, and the phrasing has been carefully adjusted to suit wind and string players. Since these are vocal selections, they must be played in a very lyrical and expressive manner, with special attention paid to phrasing and breathing. In addition, I have taken special care in arranging these pieces so as to be true to Copland's compositional style and techniques. These solos serve as an excellent introduction to twentieth century musical style for young musicians and give them a chance to experience the music of Aaron Copland, America's definitive composer.

Good luck, and I hope that you enjoy the solos!!!

Quincy C. Hilliard, Ph.D.
University of Southwestern Louisiana

Préface

C'est avec plaisir que j'ai élaboré cette série de recueils de solos basés sur la musique d'Aaron Copland. Un grand nombre d'entre eux ont été tirés de ses œuvres vocales et le phrasé a été soigneusement ajusté pour convenir aux joueurs d'instruments à vent et à cordes.

Étant donné qu'il s'agit de sélections vocales, elles doivent être jouées de façon très lyrique et expressive, en faisant particulièrement attention au phrasé et à la reprise du souffle. En outre, je me suis efforcé de rester proche du style et des techniques de composition de Copland quand j'ai arrangé ces morceaux. Les solos constituent pour les jeunes musiciens une excellente introduction au style musical du XXᵉ siècle et leur donnent l'occasion d'apprécier la musique d'Aaron Copland, compositeur américain par excellence.

Bonne chance, j'espère que vous apprécierez ces solos!!!

Quincy C. Hilliard, Ph.D.
Université du sud-ouest de la Louisiane

Vorwort

Es war mir eine große Freude, diese Sammlung von Solos, die in der Musik Aaron Coplands ihren Ursprung haben, zusammenzustellen. Viele dieser Solos stammen aus Coplands Werken für Singstimmen, und die Phrasierung wurde sorgfätig an die Anforderungen für Blas- und Streichinstrumente angepaßt.

Da diese Stücke für Singstimmen komponiert wurden, müssen sie sehr lyrisch und ausdrucksvoll gespielt werden, wobei der Phrasierung und der Atemtechnik besondere Aufmerksamkeit zu schenken ist. Außerdem war es mir besonders daran gelegen, diese Stücke so zu arrangieren, daß sie Coplands Kompositionsstil und -technik treugeblieben sind. Diese Solos sind für junge Musiker eine ausgezeichnete Einführung in den musikalischen Stil des zwanzigsten Jahrhunderts und bieten eine gute Gelegenheit, die Musik Aaron Coplands, des ausgesprochen amerikanischen Komponisten, zu erleben.

Alles Gute, und ich hoffe, daß Sie an den Solos Ihre Freude haben!!!

Quincy C. Hilliard, Ph. D.
University of Southwestern Louisiana

Prefacio

Me complace haber completado esta serie de partituras para solista, basadas en la música de Aaron Copland. Muchos de estos arreglos se inspiran en las composiciones para canto de Copland, y la fraseología ha sido cuidadosamente ajustada para adaptarla a los instrumentos de viento y de cuerda.

Como estas selecciones son para canto, se las debe interpretar en forma altamente lírica y expresiva, prestando particular atención a la fraseología y la respiración. Además, he puesto gran cuidado en mantener la fidelidad al estilo y las técnicas de composición de Copland en el arreglo de estas piezas. Estos libros para solistas constituyen una excelente introducción al estilo musical del siglo XX para jóvenes músicos, permitiéndoles experimentar la música de Aaron Copland, el compositor por excelencia de Estados Unidos.

¡Buena suerte, y espero que disfruten de estas partituras para solistas!

Quincy C. Hilliard, Ph.D.
Universidad de Southwestern Louisiana

Aaron Copland
b. Brooklyn, New York November 14, 1900;
d. Peekskill, New York December 2, 1990

Aaron Copland's name is, for many, synonymous with American music. It was his pioneering achievement to break free from Europe and create a concert music that is recognizably, characteristically American. In addition to writing such well-loved works as *Fanfare for the Common Man, Rodeo,* and *Appalachian Spring,* Copland conducted, organized concerts, wrote popular books on music, and served as an American cultural ambassador to the world.

Following early studies in piano and harmony, at the age of 20 Copland left New York for Paris. It was there, in the course of studies with his teacher and mentor Nadia Boulanger, that he became interested in incorporating popular styles into his music. Upon his return to the U.S. in 1924 he achieved immediate renown with his angular, dissonant *Organ Symphony;* further success followed with works such as his jazz-tinged *Music for the Theater.* At the same time, he advanced the cause of new music through lectures and writings, and organized the famed Copland-Sessions concerts, which introduced many important works of the European avant-garde to U.S. audiences for the first time.

As America entered first a Depression, and then a war, Copland began to share many of his fellow artists' commitment to capturing a wider audience and speaking to the concerns of the average citizen in those times of trouble. His intentions were fulfilled as works from *Billy the Kid* to *Lincoln Portrait* to the Pulitzer Prize-winning *Appalachian Spring* found both popular success and critical acclaim. Later, he turned to an individualized 12-tone compositional technique. His orchestral works *Connotations* (1962) and *Inscape* (1967) stand as perhaps the definitive statements of his mature modernist style.

Aaron Copland was one of the most honored cultural figures in the history of the United States. The Presidential Medal of Freedom, the Kennedy Center Award, the National Academy of Motion Picture Arts and Sciences "Oscar", and the Commander's Cross of the Order of Merit of the Federal Republic of Germany were only a few of the honors and awards he received. In addition, he founded or led several important arts organizations, and received honorary doctorates from more than 40 colleges and universities. In 1982, The Aaron Copland School of Music was established in his honor at Queens College of the City University of New York.

Aaron Copland

né à Brooklyn (New York) le 14 novembre 1900

décédé à Peekskill, New York le 2 décembre 1990

Pour bien des gens, Aaron Copland est synonyme de musique américaine. Il fit œuvre de pionnier en cherchant à se libérer de l'influence européenne et à créer une musique de concert qui soit typique et caractéristique de l'Amérique. Il a composé des œuvres très appréciées comme *Fanfare for the Common Man, Rodeo* et *Appalachian Spring* et a également dirigé des orchestres, organisé des concerts, écrit des livres populaires sur la musique et servit d'ambassadeur culturel de l'Amérique dans le monde entier.

Copland étudia très tôt le piano et l'harmonie puis, à l'âge de 20 ans, il quitta New York pour Paris. C'est là, durant ses études avec Nadia Boulanger, son professeur et mentor, qu'il commença à incorporer des styles populaires dans sa musique. Lorsqu'il retourna aux Etats-Unis en 1924, il se fit immédiatement un nom grâce à sa *Symphonie pour orgue,* angulaire et dissonante ; son succès se poursuivit avec des morceaux, comme *Music for the Theater,* une œuvre teintée de jazz. En même temps, il fit progresser l'acceptation de la nouvelle musique en donnant des conférences et en écrivant des articles et il organisa les fameux concerts Copland-Sessions qui présentèrent pour la première fois au public américain un grand nombre d'importantes œuvres européennes d'avant-garde.

Au moment de la Dépression, puis quand l'Amérique entra en guerre, Copland, comme ses collègues, chercha à toucher un public plus vaste en traitant des sujets de préoccupations de l'individu moyen dans ces moments difficiles. Il atteignit ses objectifs lorsque *Billy the Kid, Lincoln Portrait* et *Appalachian Spring* - qui remporta le prix Pulitzer - connurent un succès à la fois populaire et critique. Par la suite, il adopta une technique de composition individuelle dodécaphone. Ses œuvres orchestrales *Connotations* (1962) et *Inscape* (1967) symbolisent sans doute le style moderniste de sa maturité.

Aaron Copland fut l'une des personnalités culturelles les plus honorées de l'histoire des Etats-Unis. Parmi les honneurs et les récompenses qui lui furent attribués, on compte : The Presidential Medal of Freedom (La Médaille présidentielle de la Liberté), le Kennedy Center Award (Prix du Centre Kennedy), l'Oscar de la National Academy of Motion Picture Arts and Sciences (Académie nationale des arts et des sciences cinématographiques), ainsi que la Croix de Commandeur de l'Ordre du Mérite de la République fédérale d'Allemagne. En outre, il fonda ou dirigea d'importantes organisations artistiques et reçut des doctorats honorifiques de plus de 40 universités. En 1982, l'école de musique Aaron Copland fut créée en son honneur au Queens College de la City University of New York.

Aaron Copland
Geboren in Brooklyn, New York, am 14. November 1900;
Gestorben in Peekskill, New York, am 2. Dezember 1990

Für viele ist der Name Aaron Copland gleichbedeutend mit amerikanischer Musik. Es ist seiner Pionierarbeit zu verdanken, daß sich die amerikanische Konzertmusik vom europäischen Einfluß abgewandt und deutlich amerikanische Eigenschaften angenommen hat. Copland hat nicht nur beliebte Werke wie *Fanfare for the Common Man, Rodeo,* und *Appalachian Spring* geschaffen, er hat auch Konzerte dirigiert und organisiert, populäre Bücher über Musik geschrieben und der ganzen Welt als Botschafter der amerikanischen Kultur gedient.

Nach dem frühen Studium des Klaviers und der Harmonie ist Copland mit zwanzig Jahren von New York nach Paris umgezogen. Im Laufe seines dortigen Studiums unter Nadia Boulanger, seiner Lehrerin und Mentorin, begann er mit einem volkstümlichen Stil für seine Musik. Nach seiner Rückkehr in die U.S.A. im Jahre 1924 wurde er schnell durch seine widerspenstige, dissonante Orgelsymphonie (Organ Symphony) bekannt; weiterhin trugen Werke wie seine jazz-beeinflußte Theatermusik (Music for the Theater) zu seinem Erfolg bei. Gleichzeitig unterstützte er moderne Musik durch Vorträge und Schriften und organisierte die berühmten Copland-Konzerte "Copland Sessions", wo viele Kompositionen der europäischen Avantgarde dem amerikanischen Publikum erstmalig zu Gehör kamen.

Während der Depressionsjahre in Amerika, denen bald ein Krieg folgte, fühlte Copland gleich anderen Künstlern die Verpflichtung, eine breitere Zuhörerschaft und die Interessen der Alltagsmenschen in diesen unruhigen Zeiten anzusprechen. Er realisierte seine Ideen in Werken wie *Billy the Kid* und dem *Lincoln Portrait* bis hin zu *Appalachian Spring* (dieses Werk wurde mit dem Pulitzerpreis ausgezeichnet), die sowohl allgemeinen Erfolg als auch kritischen Beifall fanden. Später wandte er sich einer individualisierten Zwölfton-Kompositionstechnik zu. Seine Orchesterstücke *Connotations* (1962) und *Inscape* (1967) können wohl als ein definitives Manifest seines reifen, modernen Stils betrachtet werden.

Aaron Copland war eine der meist geehrten Persönlichkeiten in der Kulturgeschichte der Vereinigten Staaten. Unter seinen Auszeichnungen und Preisen sind die Presidential Medal of Freedom, die Kennedy Center Award, der "Oskar" der National Academy of Motion Picture Arts and Sciences und das Bundesverdienstkreuz der deutschen Bundesrepublik zu nennen. Außerdem hat er mehrere wichtige Organisationen für die Künste gegründet bzw. geleitet und hat von über 40 Colleges und Universitäten Doktortitel h. c. erhalten. 1982 wurde ihm zu Ehren die Aaron Copland School of Musikschule am Queens College der City University of New York gegründet.

Aaron Copland

Nacido en Brooklyn, Nueva York, el 14 de noviembre de 1900;

Fallecido en Peekskill, Nueva York, el 2 de diciembre de 1990

El nombre de Aaron Copland es, para muchos, el sinónimo mismo de la música estadounidense. En una acometida verdaderamente pionera, él supo desligarse de Europa, creando música seria con características estadounidenses netamente reconocibles. Además de componer obras tan renombradas como *la Fanfarria para el hombre común, Rodeo* y *Appalachian Spring,* Copland dirigió orquestas, organizó conciertos, escribió libros de gran difusión sobre música, y se desempeñó como embajador de la cultura estadounidense en el mundo entero.

Después de estudiar el piano cuando muy joven y tomar cursos de armonía, Copland salió de Nueva York, a los veinte años de edad, rumbo a París. Allí, mientras estudiaba con su maestra y mentora Nadia Boulanger, empezó a interesarse por incorporar en su música estilos populares. A su regreso a los Estados Unidos, en 1924, alcanzó un renombre inmediato con su angular y disonante *Sinfonía para órgano;* el éxito siguió acompañándole con los matices de jazz de su composición *Música para el teatro.* Al mismo tiempo, fomentó el reconocimiento de la música contemporánea mediante conferencias y escritos, y organizó los afamados conciertos llamados "Copland-Sessions", que presentaban al público estadounidense, por primera vez, numerosas obras importantes de la *avant-guarde* europea.

Mientras el país pasaba por los momentos difíciles de una depresión primero y luego de una guerra, Copland comenzó a compartir el anhelo de muchos otros artistas por captar una audiencia más amplia, dirigiéndose a las preocupaciones del hombre común. Evidentemente, cumplió con sus intenciones, pues sus obras como *Billy the Kid, Retrato de Lincoln,* y *Appalachian Spring,* que fuera merecedora del premio Pulitzer, hallaron éxito de público y de crítica a la vez. Más adelante, adoptó una técnica de composición personalizada de 12 tonos. Sus obras para orquesta *Connotations* (1962) e *Inscape* (1967) representan tal vez la manifestación definitiva de su estilo modernista maduro.

Aaron Copland fue una de las figuras culturales más reconocidas en la historia de los Estados Unidos. La Medalla presidencial de la libertad, el Premio del Centro Kennedy, el "Oscar" de la Academia nacional de artes y ciencias cinematográficas, y la Cruz de Comendador en la Orden del Mérito de la República Federal Alemana son sólo algunos de los honores y galardones que mereció. Además, fundó o dirigió varias organizaciones artísticas de importancia, y recibió doctorados *honoris causa* de más de 40 facultades y universidades. En 1982 la Facultad de música Aaron Copland fue fundada en su honor en el Colegio universitario de Queens de la Universidad de la Ciudad de Nueva York.

Biography

Quincy C. Hilliard, Ph.D.
Quincy C. Hilliard's compositions for wind band are performed throughout the United States and those parts of the world where there are wind bands of the British-American instrumentation. He is frequently commissioned by conductors for new compositions, and has been a nine-time recipient of the distinguished American Society for Composers, Authors and Publishers (ASCAP) award recognizing the numerous performances of his works. Dr. Hilliard's stature as an outstanding conductor and educator is apparent as he is invited to all parts of North America and Australia to conduct, adjudicate festivals, and demonstrate effective teaching techniques. He was commissioned by the Cultural Olympiad of the Atlanta Committee for the Olympic Games to write a composition for the 1996 Olympics. He has also written the music score for a film documentary entitled "The Texas Rangers" for public television. In the spring of 1997, Dr. Hilliard was appointed by the Governor of Louisiana to the Louisiana Arts Council.

Dr. Hilliard has extensive pedagogical publications in journal articles and books which include *Skill Builders Books 1* and *2*. Also, he is a recognized scholar of the music of Aaron Copland. He serves as a consultant/clinician/conductor for Boosey & Hawkes Publishers and Carl Fischer Publishers. Dr. Hilliard is also the president of Hilliard Music Enterprises, Inc. a personal consulting firm which has a corporate board of distinguished music educators. He is currently associate professor of music theory and composition at the University of Southwestern Louisiana in Lafayette, and holds the Heymann Endowed Professorship.

Biographie

Quincy C. Hilliard, PhD
Les compositions de Quincy C. Hilliard pour harmonies sont jouées dans tous les États-Unis et les parties du monde où il existe des harmonies composées d'instruments à vent anglo-américains. Des chefs d'orchestre lui commandent fréquemment de nouvelles œuvres et il a reçu neuf fois le prix de la Société américaine des compositeurs, auteurs et éditeurs (ASCAP), témoignant du grand nombre de fois où ses œuvres ont été exécutées. En raison de sa grande réputation comme chef d'orchestre et éminent éducateur, le Dr. Hilliard est invité partout en Amérique du Nord et en Australie pour diriger des orchestres, faire partie de jurys à des festivals, et démontrer des techniques pédagogiques efficaces. L'Olympiade culturelle du Comité des Jeux olympiques à Atlanta lui a commandé une œuvre pour les Jeux de 1996. Il a également écrit la musique du documentaire intitulé *The Texas Rangers* pour une chaîne de télévision publique. Au printemps 1997, le Dr. Hilliard a été nommé membre du Conseil des arts de Louisiane par le Gouverneur de l'État.

Parmi les nombreuses œuvres pédagogiques du Dr. Hilliard, on compte des articles dans des revues et des livres dont *Skill Builders Books 1* and *2*. Il est également reconnu comme un spécialiste de la musique d'Aaron Copland. Il est consultant-professeur de cours pratiques-chef d'orchestre chez Boosey & Hawkes Publishers et Carl Fischer Publishers. Le Dr. Hilliard est aussi directeur général de Hilliard Music Enterprises, Inc., un cabinet de consultant individuel dont le conseil d'administration est composé d'éminents professeurs de musique. Il est actuellement professeur de théorie et de composition musicale à l'Université du sud-ouest de la Louisiane à Lafayette et détient la chaire fondée par Heymann.

Biographie

Quincy C. Hilliard, Ph. D.
Quincy C. Hilliards Kompositionen für Blasorchester werden überall in den Vereinigten Staaten und in Gebieten der Welt aufgeführt, wo es Blasorchester für britisch-amerikanische Instrumentierung gibt. Dirigenten beauftragen ihn häufig mit neuen Kompositionen, und er hat bereits neunmal die distinguierende Auszeichnung der (American Society for Composers, Authors and Publishers [ASCAP]) in Anerkennung der großen Anzahl von Aufführungen seiner Werke erhalten. Hilliards Ruf als hervorragender Dirigent und Ausbilder kommt darin zum Ausdruck, daß er überall in Nordamerika sowie Australien zum Dirigieren, zur Beurteilung von Festspielen und zur Demonstration effektiver Lehrtechniken berufen wird. Er wurde von der "Cultural Olympiad of the Atlanta Committee for the Olympic Games" mit einer Komposition für die olympischen Spiele 1996 beauftragt. Auch hat er die Musik für einen Dokumentarfilm "The Texas Rangers" für öffentliches Fernsehen geschaffen. Im Frühjahr 1997 wurde Hilliard vom Gouverneur von Louisiana zum Mitglied des *Louisiana Arts Council* ernannt.

Pädagogische Abhandlungen von Hilliard wurden weitgehend.in Zeitschriften und Büchern veröffentlicht, darunter *Skill Builders Books 1* and *2*. Auch wird er als Kenner von Aaron Coplands Musik geschätzt. Er ist Berater/Helfer/Dirigent für die Verlage Boosey & Hawkes Publishers und Carl Fischer. Außerdem ist Hilliard Präsident der Hilliard Music Enterprises, Inc., einer Firma für persönliche Beratung, deren Vorstandsmitglieder berühmte Musikpädagogen sind. Er ist z. Zt. außerordentlicher Professor für Musiktheorie und Komposition an der University of Southwestern Louisiana in Lafayette und hat den Lehrstuhl der Heyman-Stiftung inne.

Bíografía

Quincy C. Hilliard, Ph.D.
Las composiciones de Quincy C. Hilliard para conjuntos de instrumentas de viento se interpreta en todos los Estados Unidos y en aquellas regiones del mundo donde existen conjuntos de instrumentos de viento de instrumentación angloamericana. Muchos directores de orquesta le comisionan con frecuencia composiciones nuevas y mereció nueve veces el distinguido galardón de la Asociación estadounidense de compositores, autores y editores (American Society for Composers, Authors and Publishers [ASCAP]), en reconocimiento de las numerosas interpretaciones de sus obras. La estatura del Dr. Hilliard como destacado director de orquesta y educador se desprende de las invitaciones que recibe de todas las regiones de Norteamérica y Australia para dirigir orquestas, actuar como juez en festivales y demostrar técnicas eficaces de enseñanza. El comité cultural de las Olimpiadas para los Juegos olímpicos en Atlanta le comisionó una obra para las Olimpiadas de 1996. También compuso la partitura de la película documental titulada "The Texas Rangers" para la televisión pública. En la primavera de 1997, el Dr. Hilliard fue nombrado miembro del Consejo para las artes de Louisiana por el gobernador del estado de Louisiana.

El Dr. Hilliard ha publicado numerosas obras pedagógicas en revistas especializadas, así como varios libros, entre ellos *Skill Builders Books 1* y *2*. Al mismo tiempo se lo reconoce como una autoridad en el sector de la música de Aaron Copland. Presta servicios como asesor, clínico y director de orquesta en las editoriales Boosey & Hawkes y Carl Fischer. El Dr. Hilliard es el presidente de Hilliard Music Enterprises, Inc., una empresa de asesoría personal que cuenta con una junta directiva integrada por distinguidos educadores en el campo de la música. Actualmente es profesor adjunto de teoría de la música y composición en la Universidad de Southwestern Louisiana en Lafayette, y ocupa la cátedra dotada por Heymann.

SIMPLE GIFTS
Shaker Song *from* OLD AMERICAN SONGS, Set 1

Flute

I'VE HEARD AN ORGAN TALK SOMETIMES
from TWELVE POEMS OF EMILY DICKINSON

VIEUX POÉME
(Old Poem)

Flute

I BOUGHT ME A CAT
from OLD AMERICAN SONGS, Set 1

Flute

LAURIE'S SONG
from the opera THE TENDER LAND

Flute

BILLY AND HIS SWEETHEART
from BILLY THE KID

Flute

DIRGE IN WOODS

Flute

Boosey & Hawkes, Inc., Sole Publisher and Licensee.   M-051-59173-2

ZION'S WALLS
Revivalist Song *from* OLD AMERICAN SONGS, Set 2

Flute

CHING-A-RING CHAW
Minstrel Song *from* OLD AMERICAN SONGS, Set 2

Flute

THE LITTLE HORSES
Lullaby *from* OLD AMERICAN SONGS, Set 2

Flute

GOING TO HEAVEN!
from TWELVE POEMS OF EMILY DICKINSON

Flute

FANFARE FOR THE COMMON MAN

Flute

Aaron Copland

Aaron Copland's music is characteristically and recognizably American. Copland's untiring efforts to ensure that his works would speak to the average citizen as well as to his fellow artists made him one of the most honored cultural figures in United States history. Among countless awards and honors, Copland received the Pulitzer Prize and the Presidential Medal of Freedom. This exciting series of arrangements offers soloists the opportunity to experience some of Copland's pioneering musical achievements in the establishment of a uniquely American idiom.

La musique d'Aaron Copland est typiquement et clairement américaine. Ses efforts inlassables pour s'assurer que ses œuvres toucheraient aussi bien l'individu moyen que ses collègues en ont fait l'une des personnalités culturelles les plus honorées de l'histoire des États-Unis. Parmi les nombreuses récompenses et distinctions qui lui ont été décernées, citons le Prix Pulitzer et la Presidential Medal of Freedom. Cette remarquable série d'arrangements instrumentaux permet aux solistes d'apprécier certains des efforts de pionnier de Copland pour créer un mode d'expression musicale typiquement américain.

Die Musik Aaron Coplands ist charakteristisch und zweifellos amerikanisch. Aufgrund seiner dauernden Bemühungen, durch seine Werke sowohl den Durchschnittsmenschen als auch andere Künstler anzusprechen, wurde er zu einer der meist ausgezeichneten Persönlichkeiten in der Kulturgeschichte der Vereinigten Staaten. Unter zahllosen Preisen und Ehrenauszeichnungen, die Copland erhielt, sind auch der Pulitzerpreis und die Presidential Medal of Freedom. Diese äußerst anregende Sammlung von instrumentalen Arrangements bietet Solisten die Gelegenheit, etwas von Coplands musikalischer Pionierarbeit durch einmalige amerikanische Themen zu erleben.

La música de Aaron Copland es de carácter netamente estadounidense. Los esfuerzos incansables de Copland para que sus creaciones se dirigieran tanto al hombre común como a los artistas, lo convirtieron en una de las figuras culturales más galardonadas de la historia de los Estados Unidos. Entre incontables premios y galardones, Copland también mereció el Premio Pulitzer y la Medalla presidencial de la libertad. Esta excelente serie de arreglos instrumentales ofrece a los solistas la oportunidad de experimentar por sí mismos algunos de los logros musicales pioneros de Copland hacia el establecimiento de un lenguaje netamente estadounidense.

COPLAND INSTRUMENTAL SERIES:

Flute	M-051-59173-2
Oboe	M-051-66075-9
Clarinet	M-051-58224-2
Bassoon, Trombone, Baritone B.C.	M-051-57025-6
Alto Saxophone	M-051-68068-9
Baritone Saxophone	M-051-68069-6
Horn	M-051-04033-9
Trumpet, Tenor Sax, Baritone T.C.	M-051-01086-8
Tuba	M-051-02029-4
Violin	M-051-35182-4
Viola	M-051-49056-1
Cello	M-051-37211-9
Bass	M-051-36023-9
Piano Accompaniment	M-051-24616-8

U.S. $11.99
M-051-59173-2

BOOSEY & HAWKES

AN IMAGEM COMPANY

Distributed By
HAL•LEONARD®

ISBN-13: 978-1-4234-6157-

Distributed By
HAL LEONARD

0 73999 72885 9
HL48005951

48005951   9 781423 461579